British Legends: The Life and Legacy of Margaret Thatcher

By Charles River Editors

About Charles River Editors

Charles River Editors was founded by Harvard and MIT alumni to provide superior editing and original writing services, with the expertise to create digital content for publishers across a vast range of subject matter. In addition to providing original digital content for third party publishers, Charles River Editors republishes civilization's greatest literary works, bringing them to a new generation via ebooks.

Visit charlesrivereditors.com for more information.

Introduction

Margaret Hilda Thatcher (1925-)

"Being powerful is like being a lady. If you have to tell people you are, you aren't." – Margaret Thatcher

A lot of ink has been spilled covering the lives of history's most influential figures, but how much of the forest is lost for the trees? In Charles River Editors' British Legends series, readers can get caught up to speed on the lives of Great Britain's most important men and women in the time it takes to finish a commute, while learning interesting facts long forgotten or never known.

Sir Winston Churchill is often cited as Britain's greatest prime minister for leading the United Kingdom against Hitler's Nazi war machine during World War II, and indeed he was the idol of the one person who many think might have surpassed him: Margaret Thatcher. Thatcher not only became Britain's first female prime minister, she also became its longest serving prime minister.

The political precedents Thatcher set as a woman would be enough of a legacy in its own right, but Thatcher effectively wielded her power in a way that made a lasting contribution both to geopolitics and the perception of female politicians in general. Thatcher is widely credited, along with Ronald Reagan, as one of the principal Cold Warriors who brought about the demise of the Soviet Union, whose leaders gave her the famous nickname "Iron Lady". And of course, Thatcher was recently in the spotlight again with the release of the critically acclaimed movie *The Iron Lady*, starring Meryl Streep.

With the success of that movie, Thatcher has undergone a cultural revival and re-iconization in many quarters for her political stances and political achievements. At the same time, however, the role she played as a woman is now often overlooked out of the expedience of political correctness, and it is considered uncivil to analyze Thatcher's political rise through the prism of sex. In fact, at times the former Prime Minister claimed to understand an issue better due to her sex and sometimes used her sex more subliminally

British Legends: The Life and Legacy of Margaret Thatcher details the Iron Lady's life and career, but it also humanizes her and explores the role gender played in her rise to power and ultimately her legacy. Along with pictures of important people, places, and events in her life, you will learn about Margaret Thatcher like you never have before, in no time at all.

What Made Thatcher Thatcher?

Thatcher's Birthplace

For a woman destined to blaze a new trail and become a trendsetter closely followed and mimicked in places around the world, Margaret Hilda Roberts actually grew up with a relatively modest background. Along with older sister Muriel, Margaret's childhood years were spent in Grantham, living above one of the two grocery stores owned by her father, Alfred Roberts. Described by Muriel as "always a Liberal at heart", Alfred was fairly active in his church and in local politics, eventually becoming a town Alderman. More importantly, Alfred firmly instilled both church and state in his young daughter.

By her teenage years, Margaret was very active in all facets of life, credited as a hard worker who excelled at everything from playing the piano to swimming. Most notably, she showed a keen interest in the sciences, which in the first half of the 20th century was almost universally viewed as a man's domain. Margaret Robers was already proving traditional gender roles would not be insurmountable barriers.

A chemist prior to becoming a barrister specializing in tax and financial matters (not, by any means, the "softer" side of law with demanding schedules), Thatcher had always been in androcentric environments. Even the choice to be a barrister in the elite and elitist male world reflects her can-do indomitable spirit at an early age. This was the early part of the 20th century, after all. The feminist revolution and attending legal, social, cultural and economic changes had not yet taken place. As the daughter of a grocer, Thatcher had grown up in such an environment and had developed the repartee and made her peace with being the only woman, often, in such situations. She also learned how to win effectively in such environments.

Astute observers have noted that "[o]rdering Aquascutum to revamp her entire wardrobe, she had her skirts pulled up, her décolleté lowered, and began showing more of her good legs. During Question Time, I noticed she would often rub the back of one black-stockinged calf with the other foot, presumably for the delectation of the frontbenchers sitting behind her."[1] Constantly underestimated and then surpassing the expectations in part *because* of this chronic underestimation of her professional and intellectual competence, Thatcher learned to walk a very fine line.

Even more than her erudition or professional competence, what was most underestimated — due mainly to stereotypes — was Thatcher's capacity for leadership. And her take-no-prisoners approach was so polarizing, so unexpected, so shocking, given her otherwise stereotypically feminine features such as her soft voice in her earlier years and mannerisms and clothes all her life, that this misdirected her critics in a way that Thatcher later was able to capitalize upon. The famous British polemic Christopher Hitchens once observed that "she calmly destroyed and (if you will pardon the expression) dismembered all her male rivals, from Sir Geoffrey Howe to Nigel Lawson to Sir Ian Gilmour to Jim Prior, as well as a succession of Labour challengers."[2]

A clear indicator of Thatcher's growing sense of self-confidence and her feeling of what political dominance entails, even her voice became lower and more authoritative, possibly due to coaching and almost certainly due to her own conscious need to recalibrate her strategy. But none of these traits and no amount of evolution would have been successful had Thatcher not had "powerful sexuality," combined with a hunger for power, of change, and of being the epicentre of the moment.[3] This is Margaret Thatcher's story and within it is the evolving saga of a certain kind of British woman. For the purposes of this story, whether or not Thatcher was indeed a "feminist" (as if that label confers some magical powers or authority) is a happy enigma left to others to determine to his or her own satisfaction.

A Political Career Like No Other

---

[1] G. Sheehy, "The Sexy Side of Maggie: How Thatcher Used Her Softer Quality," *The Daily Beast*, Jan. 11, 2012, *available at* <www.thedailybeast.com/articles/2012/01/09/the-sexy-side-of-maggie-how-thatcher-used-her-softer-quality.html>.

[2] C. Hitchens, "The Iron Lady's Sex Appeal"

[3] A. Burgess, "On Sex and Politics and the Charms of Mrs. Thatcher," Vanity Fair, May 1985, *available at* <http://www.vanityfair.com/culture/features/1985/05/margaret-thatcher-198505> [A. Burgess, "Charms of Mrs. Thatcher"] ("There was a sexual aura which owed something to the cunning coiffure, the smile of sound teeth, the discreet makeup, the newly fined down figure, the unaggressive chic. But such an aura can never be solely the product of the dietician's or the beautician's art. You either have strong sexuality or you haven't.").

When Thatcher was elected Member of Parliament (MP) for Finchley in 1959, not many powerful women politicians existed anywhere in the world. The Queen, as a head of state, was a notable exception, but she was also obviously not a political leader. Historically, women in politics had either been like Agrippina, who had tried to control the Roman Empire through sex; Lucrezia Borgia, who effectuated the fall of dynasties and kingdoms; or Queen Elizabeth I, whose sexual magnetism nonetheless earned her the stigma of being barren. Other than Elizabeth I, none were leaders in their own right, confronted directly with the great issues of the day. Thatcher would have to invent her own political future — and her identity.

When Thatcher began her political career, she was still in her mid-20s, running in 1950 and 1951 as a Conservative in Dartford, a safely held seat for the Labour party. Even then, she was noted primarily for the novelty she represented, both as the youngest and only female candidate in the race. During that time, she also married millionaire Denis Thatcher, who helped support both her political career and legal career. A self-described "honest-to-God right-winger", Denis was also a valuable source of political support for his wife, who agreed with him on nearly every issue.

The Thatchers in 1984

After spending the middle half of the 1950s raising her young children and steering clear of politics, the adroit Margaret began her political career anew near the end of the decade, this time opting to run for the Finchley seat, a safe Conservative seat in the House of Commons. After winning a bitterly contested campaign, MP Thatcher began a meteoric ascent, taking just 2 years to become Undersecretary at the Ministry of Pensions and National Insurance. She spent the 1960s becoming one of the most forceful spokesmen in her party.

Edward Heath appointed Thatcher Secretary of State for Education and Science in his 1970 government, for a handful of reasons. First and possibly foremost, Heath appointed her partly to include and thus to subdue a potential rival, but the appointment was also made in part because her wing of the Tory Party was strong and non-negotiable in demanding Thatcher's role in the Cabinet. Moreover, the appointment could also be attributed to Thatcher's sheer competence and brilliance, which political rivals grudgingly admired.

Heath (left), pictured with Queen Elizabeth and the Nixons

In 1975, Thatcher defeated Heath in the internal Tory Party leadership election and became Leader of the Opposition, in the process becoming the first woman ever to lead a major political party in the United Kingdom. She became prime minister after winning the 1979 general election.

How did this happen? Many members of the British electorate had become unhappy with the post-war "statist consensus" that, in the eyes of some, took free-market autonomy and economic freedom away from the market and placed it with the State. Economic moderates favoured a pluralism of power repositories that neither Labour nor Mrs. Thatcher's Tories exactly delivered. Nonetheless what did seem to matter was that while Labour policies had been rejected, Mrs. Thatcher's policies or her leadership had not been tried yet. The British public was longing for something new. Thatcher's vision of a society with greater economic aspirations for the next generation, along with her own immense charisma, won the day.

Upon becoming Prime Minister, Margaret Thatcher introduced several political and economic initiatives to reverse what economists called "stagflation" and in common political-speak what

Thatcher and many others saw as the United Kingdom's precipitous decline. Her political and economic policies stressed deregulation and the truncating of red tape (particularly of the financial sector), increasing international competitiveness, free market supply-side economics, tax decreases, adaptable labour markets, the privatization of erstwhile state-owned commercial enterprises and other public industry, artificial adjusting of the money supply to reduce inflation, and diminishing both the hard power (legal authority) and soft power (influence) of trade unions.

Even great politicians are subject to the times. Thatcher's popularity during her first several years in office decreased due to recession and high unemployment, until economic recovery and the 1982 Falklands War returned support. Thatcher was re-elected in 1983 and then for a third term in 1987, but her Community Charge (known as "poll tax")[4] was strongly and widely repudiated by the public, and her uncompromising views on the European Community were not shared by many, including several others in her own Cabinet. Just as Thatcher's rise was facilitated by her sex, so was her downfall. For an aggressive female political leader like Thatcher, second acts were not allowed. The novelty had worn out, and Thatcher left office in 1990.

From Thatcher's ashes emerged a lame-duck Tory Party under John Major's leadership from 1990 to 1997. After Major came the Labour Party dominance of Tony Blair and Gordon Brown. Thatcher's legacy was that, in her wake, even the Labour governments — much to the annoyance of leftists — followed "Thatcher-lite" programs, having rejected their *own* traditionally leftist tax and spend programs. Especially as to public attitudes concerning the British "independent nuclear deterrent,…Scotland's devolution, and…European integration" Labour largely continued to the course laid down by the Thatcher era.[5] The public wanted to stay the course; the pull of *path-dependency* had been too strong.[6]

The public appetite had not had room enough for a Margaret Thatcher the fallen and fallible *woman* Prime Minister, but many of her attitudes and approaches, if not the fine details of her policies, proved to have durability and staying power. Would the notoriously prejudiced (at the time) Tories or the general public have expressed greater patience for a male politician who had been generally successful and had the experience factor as an asset? Likely so. Social scientist after social scientist will attest that the public image of male leaders allows them to fail out in the open in ways that female leaders just are not allowed.[7] Male leaders often are allowed to be just

---

[4] The tax was introduced in Scotland in 1989 and in England and Wales in 1990. Politically, it proved to be disastrous for Mrs. Thatcher.

[5] A. F. Heath, et al., THE RISE OF NEW LABOUR: PARTY POLICIES AND VOTER CHOICES 60-61 (Oxford University Press, 2001).

[6] *Id.*, at 61.

[7] J. Baxter, THE LANGUAGE OF FEMALE LEADERSHIP 64 *et seq.* (Palgrave MacMillan, 2010)(exploring how "senior women have to carry out extra 'linguistic work' to make their mark in the boardroom"); K. Jironet, FEMALE LEADERSHIP: MANAGEMENT, JUNGIAN PSYCHOLOGY, SPIRITUALITY AND THE GLOBAL JOURNEY THROUGH PURGATORY (Routledge, 2010); A. S. Wharton, THE SOCIOLOGY OF GENDER: AN INTRODUCTION TO THEORY

leaders, whereas female leaders have to be both stereotypically female as well as stereotypically leader-like.

Thatcher's Policy Composite

Economic Philosophy

"The masochist in all men responds to the aggressive woman, and recognizes that her charm lies in the appearance of velvet and the reality of iron. Political power will never be sustained by the woman who is a frump."[8] This is recipe for a certain kind of woman, just as it is recipe for a certain kind of man. A woman with strong, even judgmental, policy positions can win, but her path will inevitably be more complicated than a similarly situated man's.

Stereotypes play into this manner of thinking, and society — spun by a like-minded media (not to mention, whoever the opposition happens to be) — is often too willing to hold women to a different standard. Even in recent years, decades after Thatcher, we have seen strong female leaders such as Hillary Rodham Clinton, Sonia Gandhi, Condoleeza Rice and Indra Nooyi endure challenges that equally competitive and aggressive men do not have to.[9] It is almost impossible to endure the glaring spotlight of being expected to be fragile and "feminine" while simultaneously showing policy acumen and the toughness to endure the hurly-burly of a rough and tumble, incompassionate political universe.

Thatcher subtly fused her sex, and the strong matriarchal authority derived from it, with her policy's philosophical foundations and began giving speeches like this one:

> The economic success of the Western world is a product of its moral philosophy and practice. *The economic results are better because the moral philosophy is superior.* Choice is the essence of ethics: if there were no choice, there would be no ethics, no good, no evil; good and evil have meaning only insofar as man is free to choose.[10]

AND RESEARCH 209 (John Wiley and Sons, 2011) (explaining that gender differences of what the public expects "may be intensified at the top.").

[8] See A. Burgess, "Charms of Mrs. Thatcher."

[9] See, *e.g.*, B. Reskin, "What's the Difference? A Comment on Deborah Rhode's 'The Difference 'Difference' Makes'" 112 *in* D. L. Rhode, THE DIFFERENCE 'DIFFERENCE' MAKES: WOMEN IN LEADERSHIP (Stanford University Press, 2003) ("men have more flexible jobs, higher rates of promotion, and more authority on the job.").

[10] M. Thatcher, Speech to Zurich Economic Society ("The New Renaissance"), The University of Zurich, Zurich, Switzerland (March 14, 1977).

Had a white male delivered the same words, he most likely would have been pilloried for Occidental-minded racism. Not only did Thatcher get away with it, she was also praised for her common sense vision. Thatcher was able to play on the "woman complex" successfully. This was the combination of a nanny state-*style* with the *substance* of anything but. From Thatcher's story, as much as we can appreciate the importance of ideas, not an insignificant take-away is that method and approach matter. Had Thatcher's ideas been delivered by a party not nearly as well-attuned to the art of persuasion, in all its forms (and not limited to the verbal), Thatcher may not have become Thatcher — and remained so, years after leaving office.

Thatcher sold many of Great Britain's nationalized industries back to private investors and cut taxes. Thatcher's influences were monetarist thinking and Milton Friedman-type economists, who urged governments to control the money supply rather than work to control demand. To a large extent, Thatcher broke the power of the trade unions, notably in the mining, print and shipbuilding industries and the public sector. Due to her uncompromising leadership style, she became known as the "Iron Lady."

The Falklands

A defining component of the Iron Lady's military legacy, of course, was the Falklands War. In April 1982, the prevailing military junta in Argentina invaded the U.K.-controlled Falkland Islands and South Georgia, thereby inducing the Falklands War. Thatcher had hit upon a landmark test of her tenure. Thatcher chaired a minuscule, informal War Cabinet (different from her usual Cabinet) to control the direction and discharge of this military action. By early April 1982, Thatcher's War Cabinet had dispatched a naval force to regain the islands for the United Kingdom.

Deeply controversial at the time, the 1982 war over the ownership of the Falkland Islands between Great Britain and Argentina allowed Thatcher to show her martial side. When Argentina invaded the Falklands, the United States found itself in a difficult situation, as both Great Britain and Argentina were its allies and trade partners. The United States initially attempted to broker a settlement, but Mrs. Thatcher rejected this compromise, thus cementing her reputation as the Uncompromiser-in-Chief. Upon this, the United States supported Britain with intelligence, not to mention the supply of advanced AIM-9L Sidewinder missiles. This invasion was preceded, and perhaps even encouraged, when Thatcher withdrew the Royal Navy's Antarctic ship HMS Endurance from the South Atlantic, thus giving Argentina what they thought was a free hand to invade.

This is where both Thatcher's *rhetoric* ("Where there is discord, may we bring harmony. Where there is error, may we bring truth. Where there is doubt, may we bring faith. And where there is despair, may we bring hope," "The lady's not for turning" or "Let Labour's Orwellian nightmare of the Left be a spur for us to dedicate with a new urgency our every ounce of energy and moral strength to rebuild the fortunes of this free nation," for example)[11] and her actions began to imitate that of a mother swan trying to protect her cygnets, Gloriana protecting her subjects from the wicked Spanish Armada or whatever other metaphor one elects to use. Thatcher spoke both like a warrior ready to go to battle as well as a peace-maker holding a dove in her hands, much like the Americans' eagle emblem with the same somewhat paradoxical but ultimately reconcilable message. The Prime Minister instantly declared her powerful intention to regain the islands and dispatched a naval task force.

With help from the Chilean President Pinochet (later to be tried as a war criminal for other transgressions) and, far more furtively, Thatcher's ally Ronald Reagan, the British forces quickly recaptured the Falklands. The confrontation that had had the potential to tear the British public apart melted away. From the war emerged a resurgence of popular rejoicing and patriotic enthusiasm, and of course Thatcher's mandate to allow council housing tenants to buy their homes. The Labour opposition was hopelessly mired with in-fighting, delivering for Thatcher a landslide victory in the June 1983 general election. The conflict also led to a strong friendship with the Chilean leader Augusto Pinochet after Chile helped Britain in the conflict.

Pinochet

The hostilities lasted only a few months. Argentina succumbed on 14 June, but Britain did suffer the deaths of 255 servicemen and 3 Falkland Islanders. In contrast, Argentina's fatalities numbered 649, half of whom were the direct result of the torpedoing and sinking by the nuclear submarine HMS Conqueror of ARA General Belgrano in May. Mrs. Thatcher was castigated by the media and some special interest groups for letting diplomatic relations as well as the Falklands' defense become fraught with ineffectiveness. She was also chastised for the military decision to sink the General Belgrano.

---

[11] "1980: Thatcher 'not for turning,'" October 10, 1980, *available at* <http://news.bbc.co.uk/onthisday/hi/dates/stories/october/10/newsid_2541000/2541071.stm>.

Ultimately, however, she was regarded to have earned her military commander *bona fides*, along the likes of her political hero, Winston Churchill. The comparison would be repeated over and over again on issue after issue. The Falklands victory and economic recuperation led to Thatcher's electoral victory in 1983. It did not hurt that the Labour Party was hopelessly divided and rather leaderless. Thatcher began to call this phenomenon the "Falklands Spirit." Some commentators and historians even suggest that Thatcher began to see the value of quick, rapid-fire choices made by the War Cabinet than the slower, more deliberative and sometimes convoluted peacetime Cabinet decisions.[12] A permanent switch, though, would have been constitutionally unthinkable and perniciously Cromwellian.[13]

Privatisation

On the social front, in 1986, Thatcher's government proscribed the promotion of homosexuality in state schools. Her actions and the philosophy leading to those actions were hailed as morally courageous and almost maternally solicitous by conservative feminists and likeminded social groups. Thatcher followed the same basic strategy when she "emancipated" trade union members by forcing union leaders to hold more democratic, secret ballot elections rather than employ any manner of coercive or wink-and-nod tactics.[14] Her chief foes in this conflict were the leaders of the National Miners' Union (NUM). Thatcher enjoyed looking like a mother-figure, and she played not only on the psyche of the dishevelled school children looking for a strong mother figure and in some cases mother substitute but also on the Virgin Mary-doting-on-Christ-Child theme.

Even Jim Prior's Employment Protection Bill as well as the civil and *criminal* law means Thatcher used (though she downplayed the criminal law usage to tame the unions) did not doom Mrs. Thatcher.[15] The tough love could be contextualized and understood better; the medicine certainly went down easier. The most ironic aspect of the whole era, now surreal, is that this late 1978-early 1979 "winter of discontent" induced, or at least not destroyed, by Mrs. Thatcher negatively affected almost everyone except Mrs. Thatcher herself. She came out on top politically. Whether it was her style, her media spin, admiration of her strength, or just politics taking its time to catch up with her slowly is a harder question and one upon which historians differ.

Undoubtedly the miners' strike was the largest confrontation ever to occur between the unions and Mrs. Thatcher. In March 1984, the National Coal Board (NCB) proposed to shut down 20 of

---

[12] M. Hastings & S. Jenkins, BATTLE FOR THE FALKLANDS 145 (Macmillan, 2010).

[13] Oliver Cromwell, Lord Protector and creator of the English Commonwealth, was instrumental in executing the Stuart monarch Charles I in 1649.

[14] C. Howell, TRADE UNIONS AND THE STATE: THE CONSTRUCTION OF INDUSTRIAL RELATIONS INSTITUTIONS IN BRITAIN, 1890-2000 187 *et seq.* (Princeton University Press, 2007).

[15] C. Wigley, BRITISH TRADE UNIONS, 1945-1995 93 (Manchester University Press, 1997).

the 174 publicly-owned mines and erase 20,000 jobs (out of 187,000), or 10.6%. Two-thirds of all British miners, led by the National Union of Mineworkers (NUM) under the famous or infamous Arthur Scargill, put down their tools as a note of protest. In her usual combative style, Thatcher refused even to meet with Scargill, let alone countenance the union's demands. She went further and compared the miners' dispute to the Falklands War, stating in a 1984 speech: "We had to fight the enemy without in the Falklands. We always have to be aware of the enemy within, which is much more difficult to fight and more dangerous to liberty." Notice, in Thatcher's words, the admonition to Britannia's prodigal or otherwise errant sons, a call to punish or even to ostracise them from society in some shape.

After a year of strikes, around the March of 1985, the leaders of the NUM retreated without a deal. The economic cost was estimated to be at least £1.5 billion. Indeed, some economists attributed the decline of the British pound against the U.S. dollar to the export decline caused by the strike. Thatcher shut down 25 unprofitable coal mines in 1985. The remaining ones were privatised in 1994. The ultimate shutting down of 150 coal mines, some of which were not necessarily sustaining losses, caused the loss of tens of thousands of jobs.

Another point about Thatcher's character emerges here: Miners were part of the anti-Heath constituency who had caused his political decline, which now gave Mrs. Thatcher all the more reason to succeed. Thatcher wanted to show up Heath but, even more, Thatcher wanted to substantiate a sameness feminist slogan: "Whatever he can do, I can do better."[16] Thatcher's initially-dubious tactics included making ready fuel stocks, selecting a strong union-busting official (Ian MacGregor), and making certain that police officers were sufficiently trained and empowered with riot-annihilating gear. It will not be known for decades how far Thatcher actually had empowered them to go in order to crush a potential impediment. Thatcher won the fight and she won the day.

Indeed, the number of stoppages reached 4,583 in 1979 (the zenith). This is when a cumulative 29 million working days were lost. In 1984, the year of the miner strike, there were 1,221, resulting in the loss of more than 27 million working days. Stoppages then fell steadily throughout the rest of Thatcher's premiership; in 1990 there were 630 and fewer than 2 million working days lost, and subsequently continued to fall. Trade union membership too declined, from 13.5 million (1979) to fewer than 10 million by 1990. The British trade union model evolved and, some would argue, was damaged by Mrs. Thatcher.

The maternal image again played up in Thatcher's dealings with the economists (and experts generally). Thatcher claimed a common-sense vision of enacting the right policy that would preclude the disincentives and promote the incentives. Thatcher saw the pernickety "rational

---

[16] The adage actually came from the Irving Berlin's 1946 song "Anything You Can Do" for the Broadway musical, *Annie Get Your Gun.*

actor" model to be clueless and often misguided.[17] Most famously, only about two economists overtly supported, while 364 opposed, Thatcher's tax-raising measure as the recession of the early 1980s deepened. By 1982, the U.K. started experiencing some signs of economic recovery, with inflation dropping to 8.6% from the earlier 18%, though unemployment was over 3 million for the first time since the Great Depression.

By 1983, total economic growth was stronger, and inflation as well as mortgage rates were low, even though output in the manufacturing sector had dropped by 30% since 1978 and unemployment continued to remain high, reaching its zenith at 3.3 million in 1984.[18] By 1987, however, unemployment was decreasing, the economy was stable and powerful, and inflation happened to be low.[19] It is anyone's (educated) guess how much these changes had to do with Mrs. Thatcher's policies or other variables. As with other politicians, Thatcher got significant amounts of both the credit and the blame.

Regarding privatisation, after Prime Minister Thatcher's 1983 election the sale of government utilities sped up. Thatcher raised £29 billion from the sale of nationalized industries, and another £18 billion from the sale of council houses. This privatisation process, especially preparing nationalised industries for privatisation, was credited by the Thatcher government claimed as greatly contributing to significant improvements in output, performance and labour productivity. The overall economic premise of Thatcher's economic philosophy, one supported by conservative intellectuals on both sides of the Atlantic, is that

> markets operate at a position very near to that which might be called 'efficient' – efficient given the costs that firms must face. It further follows from the proposition, again given the presumption of general competitiveness, that actions taken in the market by a single firm generally represent a means for advancing the interests of the firm by providing value to consumers. Put conversely, if a firm's practices did not provide value to consumers, the firm would fail in the competitive battle.[20]

---

[17] J. Blundell, MARGARET THATCHER: A PORTRAIT OF THE IRON LADY 95-96 (Algora Publishing, 2008) [J. Blundell, MARGARET THATCHER].

[18] B. Jones, et al., POLITICS UK 705-06 (Pearson Education, 2007); R. Toye & J. Gottlieb, MAKING REPUTATIONS: POWER, PERSUASION AND THE INDIVIDUAL IN MODERN BRITISH POLITICS 156-170 (I.B. Tauris Publishing, 2005) [R. Toye & J. Gottlieb, MAKING REPUTATIONS]; D. Yergin & Joseph Stanislaw, THE COMMANDING HEIGHTS: THE BATTLE FOR THE WORLD ECONOMY 14 *et seq.* (Simon and Schuster, 2002); H. Norpoth, CONFIDENCE REGAINED: ECONOMICS, MRS. THATCHER, AND THE BRITISH VOTER 9 (University of Michigan Press, 1992).

[19] R. Toye & J. Gottlieb, MAKING REPUTATIONS, *supra*, at 156-58.

[20] See G. L. Priest, *The Abiding Influence of* The Antitrust Paradox: *An Essay in Honor of Robert H. Bork*, 31 HARV. J. L. & PUB. POL'Y 455, 458 (2008) [G. L. Priest, *The Abiding Influence of* The Antitrust Paradox]; see also R. H. Bork, THE ANTITRUST PARADOX: A POLICY AT WAR WITH ITSELF (Free Press, 1978) (grounding the new competition law in consumer welfare); F. H. Easterbrook, *The Chicago School and Exclusionary Conduct*, 31 HARV. J. L. & PUB. POL'Y 439 (2008); R. A. Skitol, *The Shifting Sands of Antitrust Policy: Where it has Been,*

Certain privatised industries including the basic utilities (gas, water, and electricity), were of course natural monopolies for which privatisation meant marginal increase in competition. The privatised industries that demonstrated improvement often did so while still under public ownership. British Steel, for instance, became far more profitable while remaining a nationalised industry under the Thatcher government chairmanship of Ian MacGregor, who refused to buckle under union pressure to close plants and half the workforce.

The answer then might just be effective management rather than privatisation, but of course the Thatcherites claim that long-term effective management is unsustainable as a publicly owned industry. Regulation was also significantly expanded to compensate for the loss of direct government control, with the foundation of regulatory bodies. There is a need to point out that regulatory bodies are not that different from legislative government control, and they do not necessarily work.. It must also be pointed that Thatcherites are correct that the problem is not that the consumer is "stupid";[21] rather what few seem to have spotted is that the issue is one of informational asymmetry and the lack of time that might allow the "rational" consumer (one without significant resources) to deduce the preferred course of action accurately. On the contrary, this kind of argument in fact presupposes that the consumer is highly rational and intelligent — and far from "stupid."

Moreover, lawyers must easily see through this regulatory ruse to some extent because regulatory control is not, in practice, that different from direct ownership and control. From the perspective of the subjected industry, there is still a loss of autonomy or agency. This begs the question: To what extent were these reforms just cosmetic? Government interference with the control of a private corporation may in some cases convert "subsequent acts of the private corporation" into "acts of the State."[22]

There was no obvious, unequivocal pattern concerning competition, regulation, and

---

Where it is Now, Where it Will be in its Third Century, 9 CORNELL L. & PUB. POL'Y 239, 248 (1999).

[21] See, e.g., Jon D. Hanson & Douglas A. Kysar, *Taking Behavioralism Seriously: The Problem of Market Manipulation*, 74 N.Y.U. L. REV. 630, 633 (1999) ("These cognitive illusions—sometimes referred to as 'biases'—are not limited to the uneducated or unintelligent, and they are not readily capable of being unlearned. Instead, they affect us all with uncanny consistency and unflappable persistence." (footnotes omitted)); Christine Jolls et al., *A Behavioral Approach to Law and Economics*, 50 STAN. L. REV. 1471, 1541 (1998) ("In its normative orientation, conventional law and economics is often strongly antipaternalistic. . . . [B]ounded rationality pushes toward a sort of anti-antipaternalism—a skepticism about antipaternalism, but not an affirmative defense of paternalism."); Russell B. Korobkin & Thomas S. Ulen, *Law and Behavioral Science: Removing the Rationality Assumption from Law and Economics*, 88 CAL. L. REV. 1051, 1085 (2000).

[22] See D. D. Caron, "The Basis of Responsibility: Attribution and Other Trans-Substantive Rules" *in* THE IRAN-UNITED STATES CLAIMS TRIBUNAL: ITS CONTRIBUTION TO THE LAW OF STATE RESPONSIBILITY 168 (1998); see also R. Lillich, ed., INTERNATIONAL LAW OF STATE RESPONSIBILITY FOR INJURIES TO ALIENS 270-3 (1983); insurrections, civil wars, revolutions and armed external intervention have generated cases like *United States-Iran Hostages Case*, 19 ILM 553 (1980), or *Nicaragua v. United States*, 25 ILM 1023 (1986); C. F. Amerasinghe, STATE RESPONSIBILITY FOR INJURIES TO ALIENS 152-6 (Clarendon Press, 1967).

performance among the privatised industries; in most cases Thatcher's policy held that privatisation benefited consumers by keeping or lowering prices and improving efficiency (by limiting bureaucratic complacency). With greater consumer options, there could be threats that the critical mass would shift. In actuality, though, it is difficult to say if the results, on the whole, showed that the policies *work in the long run.* To be sure, Thatcher herself refused to go the full extent of the new competition law developments (championed by the Chicago School) when she refused to privatise the railway industry, something that her immediate successor John Major would do with largely calamitous results. Specifically, Thatcher did not quite accept the new arguments that "barriers to entry" do not exist or ultimately benefit consumers or that "small business need not be protected against large business."[23]

Northern Ireland

We cannot underestimate how Northern Ireland tested Thatcher as a politician and as a human being. Northern Ireland's Catholic/Protestant divisions were a thorn (and in some ways still are). In 1980 and 1981, Provisional Irish Republican Army (IRA) and Irish National Liberation Army (INLA) prisoners in Northern Ireland's Maze Prison conducted several hunger strikes in order to get back the status of political prisoners; this status had been taken away from them in 1976 under Labour. Bobby Sands, whose memorial still stands in Belfast, commenced the 1981 strike, declaring that he would fast until death unless prison inmates were granted better living and political conditions.[24]

---

[23] See G. L. Priest, *The Abiding Influence of* The Antitrust Paradox, *supra*, at 460.
[24] See B. O'Leary, *Mission Accomplished? Looking Back at the IRA*, 1 FIELD DAY REV. 217, 219 (2005); B. Kissane, EXPLAINING IRISH DEMOCRACY 156ff (Dublin, 2002); K. Toolis, REBEL HEARTS: JOURNEYS WITHIN THE IRA'S SOUL 28ff (London, 1995); S. Cronin, IRISH NATIONALISM: A HISTORY OF ITS ROOTS AND IDEOLOGY (London, 1980).

The Bobby Sands mural in Belfast

Thatcher vociferously refused to tolerate a return to political status for the prisoners, declaring "Crime is crime is crime; it is not political," but the British government *furtively* contacted the higher-ups of the IRA in a strong effort to bring the hunger strikes to an end.[25] Upon the deaths of Sands and several others, certain (though not nearly all) rights were restored to paramilitary prisoners; nonetheless there was no official status recognition. Indeed, Northern Irish violence worsened greatly during the hunger strikes.

Thatcher's IRA enemies had it in for her. She was almost assassinated in an IRA attempt at a Brighton hotel on October 12, 1984. In the attempt, five people were killed, including Government Minister John Wakeham's wife. Thatcher was staying at the hotel to attend the Tory Party Conference, which she insisted should open as scheduled the following day. It was going to be business as usual, possibly the most Thatcher'esque statement that could ever be made. Thatcher was sending a strong message even by that non-move of postponing or calling off the conference. She delivered her speech, a decision that was strongly supported across the political spectrum and enhanced her general popularity. There is nothing quite like a tragedy to unify the bickering factions.

Thatcher's reputation as an unflinchingly strong political leader won her political points, and her reputation as an unflinchingly strong *woman* political leader won her political points and a place in history. We will never know for certain the precise extent to which the call of history was on Thatcher's mind when she showed her characteristic insouciance and her devil-may-care attitude.

In November 1981 Thatcher and Irish Taoiseach Garret FitzGerald decided to establish and assemble the Anglo-Irish Inter-Governmental Council, a proactive and interactive forum where discussions, deliberations and meetings between the governments could take place. On November 15, 1985, Thatcher and FitzGerald signed the Hillsborough Anglo-Irish Agreement, which had the distinction of being the first instance that Britain had given the Republic of Ireland something of an advisory capacity in Northern Ireland's governance and administration. It must be noted that this decision was not without costs: as a note of protest, the Ulster Says No movement drew 100,000 people to a Belfast protest rally, Ian Gow resigned as Minister of State in Treasury, and *all* 15 Unionist MPs resigned their seats. The war-ready leader and rebel mother had shown she could also be a peace-maker of startling proportions, perhaps too far out in front politically, at least for the sake of cohesion.

---

[25] See J. Blundell, MARGARET THATCHER, *supra*, at 131 *et seq.*

The Cold War

On foreign relations, Thatcher found a kindred spirit over the issue of breaking the will and economic support of the Communists, particularly the Soviet Union: U.S. President Ronald Reagan. Reagan and Thatcher have historically been credited for bringing down the Berlin Wall and ending the Soviet Union as it had been known, but it remains unclear whether it would or would not have happened under a different chain of events. History's road-not-taken is almost always notoriously impossible to trace.[26]

The Thatchers and Reagans

While it is impossible to fully analyze to what extent the fall of Soviet communism and the aftermath (*perestroika*, etc.) can be attributed to Prime Minister Thatcher, it is nonetheless obvious that some credit is owed to her, even if it was just as a function of timing (she embraced the opportunity when she saw it and made more of it than was immediately evident could be the case). Thatcher took office in the 1970s, the penultimate decade in the four decade long history of the Cold War. Thatcher became closely aligned with American policies and particularly with President Reagan, an alliance grounded as much in a mutual distrust and dislike of communism

---

[26] C. Berlinski, THERE IS NO ALTERNATIVE: WHY MARGARET THATCHER MATTERS 47 *et seq.* (Basic Books, 2008).

as it was on shared economic interests. After all, in October 1983, when Reagan invaded Grenada, Thatcher powerfully and vociferously opposed him. Scholars such as Judith Resnik identify such attitudes of "form[ing] connections and groups" and "shar[ing] work stemm[ing] from" the constructive motivation "to alter the shape and understanding" of politics, life, and culture peculiarly feminine.[27]

In Thatcher's first year as Prime Minister she had indeed supported the North Atlantic Treaty Organization's (NATO) decision to deploy United States nuclear cruise missiles in Western Europe, and she had even actively enabled the United States to station 160 cruise missiles in the United Kingdom. She had stood her ground despite massive opposition by the lobbying efforts of the powerful Campaign for Nuclear Disarmament. Thatcher subsequently purchased from Reagan and the United States, as part of her pre-emptive strategy, the Trident nuclear missile submarine system. This striking move tripled Britain's nuclear forces, thereby costing more than £12 billion.[28]

Thatcher's preference to stay the course was tested (and so was her commitment to military commitments and alliances with the United States) in the Westland affair of January 1986. At that time, Thatcher allowed the struggling helicopter manufacturer Westland to reject an acquisition offer from the Italian company Agusta in favour of the management's preferred course of action. Thatcher's own Defense Secretary, Michael Heseltine, who had been a champion of the Agusta option, resigned to register his opposition to Thatcher on what he saw as this significant issue.

Other Foreign Relations

What of apartheid South Africa? Despite maintaining her anti-apartheid stance, Thatcher believed the sanctions imposed on South Africa by the Commonwealth and the European Community were ineffective. She tried to continue trade and investments with South Africa's apartheid government while convincing the regime to repudiate apartheid.[29] Thatcher's public and ostensible argument was not that different from her economic policy premise: boycotts hurt the British manufacturing works as well as poor, black South Africans. The rationale was grounded in consumer and plebeian welfare. Thatcher, perhaps due to her own personal IRA experience in Brighton, was antagonized by the tactics of the African National Congress (ANC), which Thatcher may have dismissed as "a typical terrorist organisation."[30]

---

[27] J. Resnik, "Women, Meeting (Again), in and Beyond the United States" 205 *in* D. L. Rhode, THE DIFFERENCE 'DIFFERENCE' MAKES: WOMEN IN LEADERSHIP (Stanford University Press, 2003).

[28] The 2012 cost would be approximately £17.64 billion.

[29] T. Bell & D. B. Ntsebeza, UNFINISHED BUSINESS: SOUTH AFRICA, APARTHEID, AND TRUTH 77 (Verso, 2003); J. Gardner, POLITICIANS AND APARTHEID: TRAILING IN THE PEOPLE'S WAKE 119 (HSRC Press, 1997); S. R. Lewis, THE ECONOMICS OF APARTHEID 38-52 (Council on Foreign Relations, 1990).

[30] G. Howe, CONFLICT OF LOYALTY 123-4 (Macmillan, 1994). Prime Minister Thatcher's own Foreign Secretary, Geoffrey Howe so articulated.

This impatience with agents Thatcher saw as ill in method and form as well as an effort to be expedient applied also to the Khmer Rouge government of Cambodia. Thatcher supported their retaining their United Nations seat ("the more reasonable" of the choices, she said) *after* the Cambodian-Vietnamese War saw to their ouster from Cambodia.[31]

Now we come to the Libya and Middle East issue. In April 1986, Thatcher permitted U.S. fighter and bomber jets to use the U.K.'s Royal Air Force bases to bomb of Libya in order to retaliate against the alleged Libyan bombing of a Berlin nightclub. Both Thatcher and Reagan had referred to the United Nations Charter's Article 51 allowing nations to defend themselves, sometimes pre-emptively. The move was extremely damaging and unpopular with the British public. By this time, the public was a weary one, unwilling to give Mrs. Thatcher the benefit of doubt any longer. When, as we soon shall see, she did fall from grace, it was after 11 and a half years in political office and the public patience was wearing thin. Had she served much longer, a long-tenure precedent might have been set that made room for casual corruption and other political machine-like behaviour.[32]

When Iraq's Saddam Hussein invaded Kuwait in August 1990 (mainly for oil — an interest both for the United States and the United Kingdom), Thatcher powerfully urged United States President George H. W. Bush to intervene, specifically to deploy American troops in the Middle East to oust the Iraqi military from Kuwait. Despite Bush's reluctance, Thatcher pushed him very hard and eventually won his support. In this endeavour, Thatcher provided the United States with British military forces to the international coalition in the build-up to the Gulf War, but she had resigned from office (partly *because* of this particular engagement, which may well have been a bridge too far) by the time hostilities began on January 17, 1991.

As we have seen many times over, Thatcher the peace-maker travelled alongside Thatcher the martial leader and war-monger, one of the many internal contradictions that makes the former Prime Minister's composite so interesting to study. Margaret Thatcher was among the first Western leaders to encourage to the Soviet reformer Mikhail Gorbachev. Many other Western leaders were rather lukewarm or taking longer to warm up to Gorabchev. Subequent to the Reagan–Gorbachev summit and Gorbachev's domestic reforms, in 1988 Thatcher announced that the Cold War was effectively over and that the West and the Soviet Union now enjoyed a "new relationship much wider than the Cold War ever was." Initially Thatcher strongly opposed to Germany's reunification, predicting to Gorbachev that it "would lead to a change to post-war borders, and we cannot allow that because such a development would undermine the stability of

---

[31] T. Fawthorp, GETTING AWAY WITH GENOCIDE?: ELUSIVE JUSTICE AND THE KHMER ROUGE 69-72 (UNSW Press, 2005); C. Etcheson, AFTER THE KILLING FIELDS: LESSONS FROM THE CAMBODIAN GENOCIDE 185 (Greenwood Publishing Group, 2005).

[32] It is true that Prime Minister Tony Blair (1997-2007) also served a long tenure but his tenure did not exceed Thatcher's in length.

the whole international situation and could endanger our security."

Thatcher was thinking strategically. She was concerned that a whole, united Germany would most likely choose the side of the Soviet Union and reject the NATO. Thatcher was, however, a supporter of Croatian and Slovenian independence. In a 1991 interview, Thatcher criticized the West for failing to recognize the secessionist Slovenian and Croatian republics as independent nations. Thatcher also argued that the Western powers ought to equipped Slovenia and Croatia with weapons after they were attacked by the Serbian-Yugoslav forces. Was this impartial? How would Thatcher the Prime Minister have responded had Scotland or any other part of the United Kingdom wanted total independence?[33] We may surmise that Mrs. Thatcher would not have been best pleased.

European Union

Above all else, the foreign policy stances and decisions Thatcher took and made vis-à-vis the European Community indicate that she was extraordinarily protective of British sovereignty in all matters. Her pungent dislike of European integration became ever more obvious during her Prime Minister years. The moderate stances she had once taken on this question now were miles apart from the uncompromising stance she took after her third election victory in 1987. Memorably, Thatcher explained her disagreement with almost every proposal from the European Community (EC), precursor to the European Union, for a more federal structure and greater centralisation to govern policy choices.

Back in the days of the 1975 national referendum, Thatcher and the Tories had supported (some might say, championed) British membership of the European Communities, but her views on this topic were not boundless. Thatcher saw it as a narrow question, believing that the EC's role should be confined to making sure intra-European free trade and stable, strong competition existed. Thatcher was concerned that the EC's *approach* as well as its *substantive goals* would bring about the bigger government and regulatory state she was attempting to steer the United Kingdom away from.

In 1988, Thatcher memorably remarked: "We have not successfully rolled back the frontiers of the state in Britain, only to see them re-imposed at a European level, with a European super-state exercising a new dominance from Brussels." Thatcher's now-famous Parliamentary diatribe of "No, No, No" to greater EC dominance still rings. Thatcher also was strongly opposed to the

---

[33] See, *e.g.*, R. Legvold, "Book Review: Slaughterhouse: Bosnia and the Failure of the West," *Foreign Affairs*, May/June 1995, *available at* <www.foreignaffairs.com/articles/50892/robert-legvold/slaughterhouse-bosnia-and-the-failure-of-the-west>. D. Rieff, SLAUGHTERHOUSE: BOSNIA AND THE FAILURE OF THE WEST 14 *et seq.* (Simon & Schuster, 1996); R. Ali & Lifschultz, WHY BOSNIA?: WRITINGS ON THE BALKAN WAR 112-14 (Pamphleteer's Press, 1993).

United Kingdom's membership of the Exchange Rate Mechanism, a forerunner to European Monetary Union. Her view was that such a move would limit the options for the British economy. Again, Prime Minister Thatcher stood her ground despite arguments to the contrary advanced by her Chancellor of the Exchequer Nigel Lawson and Geoffrey Howe. Nonetheless, her successor John Major convinced Thatcher to join in October 1990 — albeit at what turned out to be rather high an exchange rate.

Her Fall and Her Resurrection

Thatcher in 1990

Thatcher had led the Tories to victory in three general elections (1979, 1983 and 1987), but by 1990, Thatcher's popularity was decreasing tremendously and there were calls from within her own party for her to resign from office. She was challenged for the party leadership and just failed to gain the necessary majority in the first election, despite attaining a greater number of votes than her chief rival Michael Heseltine. Upon being persuaded by colleagues that she would narrowly fail, Thatcher decided to drop out of the second ballot and resigned as party leader on November 22, 1990.

John Major won the Tory leadership vote, and then was appointed to succeed Thatcher as Prime Minister. Thatcher was the longest serving British Prime Minister in more than a century and a half and found herself in a pantheon of two, just with the celebrated Winston Churchill. Together they remain regarded, by friend and foe alike, two of the most influential British premiers of the twentieth century. The complexity of sex played into Thatcher's political operations. There was no precedent. It was a game that she had to win once and keep winning.

Arguably Thatcher's most interesting post-Premier action came in August 1992, when Thatcher called for NATO to put a stop to the Serbian assault on Goražde and Sarajevo to end ethnic cleansing. She compared the Bosnian situation to "the worst excesses of the Nazis," and deemed this to be close to a "holocaust."[34] Thatcher made several House of Lords speeches — she had been created Baroness Thatcher —criticising the Maastricht Treaty,[35] stating bluntly (and perhaps inappropriately and presumptuously[36]) "I could never have signed this treaty." Even at her 80th birthday gala, attended by such luminaries as the Queen and then-Prime Minister Tony Blair, Mrs. Thatcher remained sharp, witty and opinionated and remained, as ever, not just a certain kind of woman but a certain kind of British woman.

Mrs. Thatcher remained a mainstay in affairs until 2002, delivering speeches, writing her own memoirs, and perhaps most famously writing about political statesmanship in *Statecraft: Strategies for a Changing World*, which she dedicated to Ronald Reagan. That all changed after she began suffering strokes in 2002, which limited her public appearances and speaking. Now well into her twilight, Thatcher is in a state of frail health, and it has been widely reported that she is suffering from dementia. Not even the Iron Lady could withstand old age.

Thatcher may be personally fading from the scene, but her reputation and legacy have never been stronger. Although *The Iron Lady* has brought her entire life, including her fight with dementia, back into the public consciousness, it's her political legacy and philosophy that have truly made her a living legend in the 21st century. In particular, her championing of free-market philosophies and her railing against government intervention at all levels, including against the European Union, have made her an icon of political conservatives across the West, elevating her onto a pedestal alongside kindred spirit Ronald Reagan. To a lesser degree, Thatcher continues to have critics, who point to high unemployment during her premiership and have charged her with doing "little to advance the political cause of women",

---

[34] M. Thatcher, "Stop the Excuses. Help Bosnia Now," *New York Times*, August 6, 1992, *available at* <http://query.nytimes.com/gst/fullpage.html?res=9E0CE7DE1731F935A3575BC0A964958260&sec=&spon=&pagewanted=2>.

[35] Treaty on European Union (92/C 191/01),

[36] Thatcher had also not had to face the particular economic and political sanctions that Tony Blair did, on behalf of the United Kingdom.

In addition to the legacy she left on Britain and Europe at large, Thatcher's life and career have left a marked legacy on all of the female politicians that have followed her since. Since the Thatcher days, female leaders have had to continue to prove their mettle as dispassionate and yet feminine, ruthless and yet maternal, fiercely intelligent to master every subtle argument and yet uphold the soft, sweeping, broad vision to encourage the troops and boost their morale. For women seeking to follow Thatcher's path, the game is still on.

Printed in Great Britain
by Amazon.co.uk, Ltd.,
Marston Gate.